THE GREAT LITTLE BOOK OF PIZZAS

top that

THE GREAT LITTLE BOOK OF PIZZAS

top that

Emma Summer

southwater

This edition is published by Southwater

Distributed in the UK by
The Manning Partnership
251–253 London Road East
Batheaston
Bath BA1 7RL
tel. 01225 852 727
fax 01225 852 852

Published in the USA by
Anness Publishing Inc.
27 West 20th Street
Suite 504
New York
NY 10011
fax 212 807 6813

Distributed in Canada by
General Publishing
895 Don Mills Road
400–402 Park Centre
Toronto, Ontario M3C 1W3
tel. 416 445 3333
fax 416 445 5991

Distributed in Australia by
Sandstone Publishing
Unit 1, 360 Norton Street
Leichhardt
New South Wales 2040
tel. 02 9560 7888
fax 02 9560 7488

Southwater is an imprint of Anness Publishing Limited
Hermes House, 88–89 Blackfriars Road, London SE1 8HA
tel. 020 7401 2077; fax 020 7633 9499

© Anness Publishing Limited 1998, 2002

Publisher Joanna Lorenz
Senior Cookery Editor Linda Fraser
Assistant Editor Sarah Ainley
Copy Editor Jenni Fleetwood
Designers Patrick McLeavey & Jo Brewer
Illustrator Anna Koska
Photographer Karl Adamson
Recipes Carla Capalbo, Shirley Gill

Previously published as *The Little Pizza Cookbook*

1 3 5 7 9 10 8 6 4 2

NOTES
For all recipes, quantities are given in both metric and imperial measures and, where appropriate, measures are also given
in standard cups and spoons. Follow one set, but not a mixture, because they are not interchangeable.

Standard spoon and cup measures are level. 1 tsp = 5ml, 1 tbsp = 15ml, 1 cup = 250ml/8fl oz

Australian standard tablespoons are 20ml. Australian readers should use 3 tsp in place of 1 tbsp
for measuring small quantities of gelatine, cornflour, salt, etc.

Contents

Introduction

It can be no accident that the pizza has become one of the world's most popular foods. What could be  more delicious than a crisp dough crust spread with a flavoursome tomato sauce, topped with your favourite ingredients and then covered in golden melted cheese? A meal in itself, served solo or with salad, pizza is enjoyed by people of all ages and is perfect for every occasion, from a child's birthday party to an after-theatre snack. Pizzettes are perfect for picnics, and calzonetti are even better, since the filling is neatly trapped inside the dough until you take that first bite.

With pizza dough so easy to make, why stake out the take-away? Just mix the ingredients, work out your frustrations on the dough and leave it to rise while you make the topping of your choice. Prepare a large quantity of the basic tomato sauce in advance, so that there will be some ready when you need it, and have a few flavoured oils handy for adding extra interest.

Experienced pizza cooks don't roll out their dough — at least, not for more than a couple of strokes. They lovingly lift, tease and stretch it to fit their tins. Mastering the art is great fun, which the whole family can enjoy, even if they only stand on the sidelines and laugh at your efforts!

A pizza party is a very successful way to entertain. Supply plenty of dough, a large selection of toppings and four or five different types of grated cheese, including mozzarella and Parmesan.

Borrow extra baking sheets, and have the oven hot before the first guests arrive. Few will be able to resist the opportunity to make their own pizza, and the kitchen will fast become the focus of the party, with friendships forming and competition hotting up over who can produce the most interesting topping.

If you are short of inspiration, just leaf through the pages of this book. Caramelized onion and salami, smoked chicken with yellow peppers, roast vegetables with goat's cheese, mussels with leeks – there is a combination for every occasion and a treat for every taste.

For a quick snack or supper, just add a topping to a French stick or ready-made base, or try a scone pizza. There is a recipe in this collection which does not even require an oven. You cook the pizza first in a pan and then finish it off under the grill.

The easiest way to cope with an unexpected influx of visitors is to offer them a tray-baked Farmhouse Pizza. The wonderful combination of tomato sauce with mushrooms, smoked ham, artichokes and anchovies, is always a favourite. Spread the topping equally over the entire pizza, or section it so that guests can avoid the ingredients they don't like.

Mini pizzas make great cocktail snacks if you add sophisticated toppings such as prawn and avocado or smoked salmon and crème fraîche. Deep-fried panzerotti – tiny turnovers – are equally popular.

Thin and crispy or deep pan indulgence, mouth-watering morsels or family feasts, pizzas never fail to rise to the occasion.

Tip-Top Toppings

ANCHOVIES

Canned anchovies make a marvellous pizza topping. They should be used straight from the drained can, but if you find them a little too salty, soak them in milk first.

ARTICHOKE HEARTS

These come canned in brine or bottled in oil. The latter are preferred for pizzas. Cut into thin slices, or chop as a filling for panzerotti.

BASIL

Known for its affinity with tomatoes, basil is a favourite pizza herb. Tear the leaves, rather than chopping them.

CAPERS

The preserved flower buds of a Mediterranean shrub, capers have a strong piquant flavour.

CHEESES

Mozzarella and Parmesan are obvious choices, but goat's cheese, Gorgonzola, Dolcelatte and mature Cheddar are also excellent. Smoked cheeses are a successful variation.

GARLIC

Garlic is added for accent, but is also wonderful as a pizza topping in its own right. Whole cloves of garlic can be roasted on top of the pizza for a marvellously mellow flavour.

MUSHROOMS

Button mushrooms are widely used (fry them first to make sure all the juices have evaporated). Try wild mushrooms too.

OLIVES

Fully ripe black olives are preferred for pizzas, providing a lovely colour contrast against the red of a rich tomato sauce.

ONIONS

Onions are usually fried before being used as a topping. Red onions look great on pizzas, especially with salami.

OREGANO

Often known as the "pizza herb", oregano can be worked into the dough or sprinkled over the topping just before baking.

PEPPERONI

An Italian cured sausage made from beef, pork and red peppers, pepperoni is available both whole and sliced in supermarkets.

PEPPERS

Strips of these brightly coloured vegetables add colour and flavour. Use peppers fresh or grill them for a special smoky taste.

PESTO

Natural basil pesto and red pesto (with added sun-dried tomatoes) are used for flavouring.

PINEAPPLE

Canned pineapple chunks are the children's favourite, especially with ham.

SWEETCORN

Drained canned sweetcorn kernels do not contribute a great deal of flavour, but add colour and texture.

TAPENADE

A paste which is made from green or black olives, ground with olive oil and seasoning, tapenade is tasty when spread on pizza bases, or spooned on top just before serving. It is especially good with goat's cheese.

TOMATOES

The absolute essential: use fresh plum or vine tomatoes, or canned chopped tomatoes. Always drain tomatoes well, though, or your pizza base will become soggy.

TOMATO PURÉE

Tomato purée is marvellous for adding extra flavour, especially to tomato sauce.

TUNA

Drained canned tuna makes a good topping and is often used on a Four Seasons pizza.

Techniques

BASIC PIZZA DOUGH
Makes one 30cm/12in base

Sift 175g/6oz/1½ cups strong white flour and 1.25ml/¼ tsp salt into a large mixing bowl. Stir in 5ml/1 tsp easy-blend dried yeast. Make a well in the centre and add 15ml/1 tbsp olive oil, with enough hand-hot water to make a soft, malleable dough. The amount will vary according to the absorbency of the flour, but you should not need more than 150ml/¼ pint/⅔ cup.

Turn the dough on to a lightly floured surface and knead for about 10 minutes, until smooth and elastic. Return it to the clean bowl. Cover with clear film and leave in a warm place for about an hour, until the dough has doubled in bulk.

Knock back the dough, turn it on to a lightly floured surface and knead again for 2–3

minutes. Roll out and use as directed, pushing up the dough edges to make a rim before adding the topping.

VARIATIONS
• *Deep-pan Pizza Dough*: Increase the amount of flour to 225g/8oz/2 cups and the salt to 2.5ml/½ tsp. Use 30ml/2 tbsp oil, but do not increase the amount of yeast.
• *Wholemeal Pizza Dough*: Use half wholemeal and half strong white flour. Add more water, if necessary.
• *Food Processor Dough*: Process the flour, salt and yeast briefly in a food processor. With the motor running, add the liquid through the feeder tube until the dough forms a soft ball. Rest for 2 minutes, then process for 1 minute to knead the dough. Put the dough in a bowl, cover and prove as for Basic Pizza Dough.

MAKING TOMATO SAUCE

Master the art of making a flavoursome tomato sauce, and not only will your pizzas taste superb, but you will have the ideal topping for pasta. Heat 15ml/1 tbsp olive oil in a saucepan and add 1 finely chopped onion with 1 crushed garlic clove. Fry over a gentle heat for 5 minutes, until softened, then add a 400g/14oz can of chopped tomatoes. Stir in 15ml/1 tbsp each of tomato purée and chopped fresh mixed herbs, with salt and pepper to taste. Add a pinch of sugar to bring out the flavour of the tomatoes.

Bring to the boil, then lower the heat and simmer, stirring occasionally, for 15–20 minutes, by which time the sauce will have reduced to a thick pulp. Leave to cool.

FLAVOURING OILS

Oil is brushed over the pizza base before the topping is added. Where appropriate, use the oil from a bottle of sun-dried tomatoes, or make your own flavoured oils.

Chilli Oil: Heat 150ml/¼ pint/⅔ cup olive oil in a saucepan until very hot, but not smoking. Carefully stir in 10ml/2 tsp tomato purée and 15ml/1 tbsp dried red chilli flakes. Leave to cool, then pour into a small jar. Cover and store in the fridge for up to 2 months (the longer you keep it the hotter it will become).

Garlic Oil: Put 4 peeled garlic cloves in a small jar. Pour in 120ml/4fl oz/½ cup olive oil. Cover the jar and store in the fridge for up to 1 month.

11

Classic Pizzas

Pizza Napoletana

INGREDIENTS

30cm / 12in pizza base
30ml / 2 tbsp olive oil
6 plum tomatoes
2 garlic cloves, chopped
115g / 4oz / ⅔ cup mozzarella cheese, grated
50g / 2oz can anchovy fillets, drained and chopped
15ml / 1 tbsp chopped fresh oregano
30ml / 2 tbsp grated Parmesan cheese
ground black pepper

SERVES 2–4

3 Mix the mozzarella cheese and anchovies in a bowl. Sprinkle the mixture over the pizza, followed by the chopped fresh oregano and Parmesan. Drizzle over the remaining oil and season with black pepper. Bake for 15–20 minutes or until the crust is crisp and golden. Serve at once.

1 Preheat the oven to 220°C/425°F/Gas 7. Brush the pizza base with 15ml/1 tbsp of the oil. Cut a small cross in the stalk end of each tomato. Place in a bowl and pour over boiling water to cover. Leave for about a minute, until the skins start to split, then drain and plunge into cold water. Gently slip off the skins.

2 Using a serrated knife, chop the tomatoes roughly. Spoon them over the pizza base to within 1cm/½ in of the rim, then sprinkle over the garlic.

13

Four Seasons Pizza

INGREDIENTS

450g/1lb peeled plum tomatoes or 2
400g/14oz cans chopped tomatoes, drained
45ml/3 tbsp olive oil
115g/4oz/1 cup mushrooms, thinly sliced
1 garlic clove, crushed
30cm/12in pizza base
350g/12oz/2 cups finely diced mozzarella cheese
4 thin slices of cooked ham, cut into 5cm/2in squares
8 stoned black olives
2 drained bottled artichoke hearts in oil, halved
5ml/1 tsp fresh oregano
salt and ground black pepper

SERVES 2–4

1 Preheat the oven to 220°C/425°F/ Gas 7. Strain the tomatoes through the medium holes of a food mill or sieve placed over a bowl, scraping in all the pulp. If you use canned tomatoes, drain them for 10 minutes before straining, or the topping will be too sloppy.

2 Heat 30ml/2 tbsp of the oil in a frying pan. Cook the mushrooms over a moderately high heat for about 5 minutes, until they are golden and most of the juices have evaporated. Stir in the garlic and set aside.

3 Then spread the tomatoes over the pizza base to within 1cm/½in of the pizza rim. Sprinkle evenly with the diced mozzarella. Using a spatula, lightly mark the pizza in quarters. Spread the mushrooms evenly over one quarter.

4 Arrange the ham squares in a second quarter and the olives and artichoke hearts on the remaining quarters. Sprinkle with oregano, salt and pepper, then drizzle the remaining olive oil over the top.

5 Bake for 15–20 minutes or until the crust is crisp and golden. Serve at once.

VARIATION

Add flaked drained tuna to the artichokes, if you like, and rounds of pepperoni to the mushrooms. The point with this pizza is that you can add whatever you like so long as the flavours do not clash.

Pizza Margherita

INGREDIENTS

30cm / 12in pizza base
30ml / 2 tbsp olive oil
1 quantity Tomato Sauce
150g / 5oz mozzarella cheese
2 ripe tomatoes, thinly sliced
6–8 fresh basil leaves
30ml / 2 tbsp grated Parmesan cheese
ground black pepper

SERVES 2–4

1 Preheat the oven to 220°C/425°F/ Gas 7. Brush the pizza base with 15ml/1 tbsp oil. Spread the tomato sauce over the base to within 1cm/ ½in of the rim.

2 Cut the mozzarella into thin slices. Then arrange the fresh tomato and mozzarella slices alternately in concentric circles on top of the pizza base.

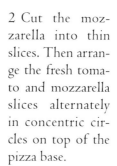

3 Tear the basil leaves roughly and sprinkle them over the pizza, then sprinkle with the Parmesan. Drizzle over the remaining olive oil and season with black pepper. Bake for 15–20 minutes or until the crust is crisp and golden. Serve at once.

Four Cheeses Pizzas

INGREDIENTS

1 quantity Basic Pizza Dough
15ml/1 tbsp Garlic Oil
½ small red onion, very thinly sliced
50g/2oz Dolcelatte cheese
50g/2oz mozzarella cheese
50g/2oz/½ cup grated Gruyère cheese
30ml/2 tbsp grated Parmesan cheese
15ml/1 tbsp chopped fresh thyme
ground black pepper

SERVES 4

3 Grind plenty of black pepper over the pizzas and bake in the oven for 15–20 minutes or until the crust on each pizza is crisp and golden. Serve at once.

1 Preheat the oven to 220°C/425°F/Gas 7. Grease two large baking sheets. Divide the dough into four pieces and roll each one out on a lightly floured surface to a 13cm/5in round. Place well apart on the greased baking sheets, then push up the edge of the dough on each round to make a thin rim.

2 Then brush each round with garlic oil and top with the red onion. Cut the Dolcelatte and mozzarella into cubes and scatter over the pizza bases. Mix the Gruyère, Parmesan and thyme in a bowl. Sprinkle the mixture over the pizzas.

17

Calzoni

INGREDIENTS

1 quantity Basic Pizza Dough
350g/12oz/1½ cups ricotta cheese
175g/6oz cooked ham, finely diced
6 tomatoes, peeled, seeded and diced
8 fresh basil leaves
175g/6oz/1 cup diced mozzarella cheese
60ml/4 tbsp grated Parmesan cheese
salt and ground black pepper
olive oil, for brushing

SERVES 4

1 Preheat the oven to 220°C/425°F/ Gas 7. Lightly grease two large baking sheets. Divide the dough into four pieces and roll each one out on a lightly floured surface to a 15cm/6in round.

2 Mix the ricotta, ham and diced tomatoes in a bowl. Tear the basil leaves roughly into pieces and add them to the bowl, with the mozzarella and Parmesan. Mix well and add plenty of salt and pepper.

3 Divide the filling equally between the four dough rounds, placing it on one half of each round and leaving a 2.5cm/1in border around the edge. Dampen the edges with a little water and fold the plain half of the dough over, as when making a Cornish pasty. Seal the edges by crimping them together with your fingers.

4 Place the calzoni on the greased baking sheets. Brush the tops lightly with olive oil and bake in the preheated oven for 15–20 minutes or until each calzone is puffed up and golden. Serve hot or cold.

COOK'S TIP

Calzoni are the perfect food for picnics and you can vary the fillings to suit the guests. For cocktail parties, you can make miniature versions, known as calzonetti.

18

Pizza Marinara

INGREDIENTS

60ml/4 tbsp olive oil
675g/1½lb plum tomatoes, peeled, seeded and chopped
30cm/12in pizza base
4 garlic cloves, cut into slivers
15ml/1 tbsp chopped fresh oregano
salt and ground black pepper

SERVES 2–4

1 Preheat the oven to 220°C/425°F/Gas 7. Heat 30ml/2 tbsp of the oil in a saucepan. Add the chopped tomatoes and cook, stirring frequently, for about 5 minutes until softened.

2 Tip the tomatoes into a sieve placed over a bowl. Leave them to drain for about 5 minutes, then transfer them to a food processor or blender. Purée until smooth.

3 Brush the pizza base with half of the remaining oil. Spoon the tomatoes over the base to within 1cm/½ in of the rim, then sprinkle with the garlic and chopped fresh oregano.

4 Then drizzle the remaining oil over the pizza and season with plenty of salt and ground black pepper. Bake the pizza in the preheated oven for 15–20 minutes or

until the crust is crisp and golden. Serve at once.

COOK'S TIP

If you are in a hurry, you can substitute two 400g/14oz cans of chopped tomatoes with herbs for the fresh tomatoes. Drain them very well for at least 10 minutes, mash them lightly in the sieve and then spread them directly on to the pizza base. There is no need to purée them first.

20

Meat & Chicken Pizzas

Prosciutto, Mushroom & Artichoke Pizza

INGREDIENTS

1 bunch spring onions
60ml/4 tbsp olive oil
225g/8oz/2 cups mushrooms, sliced
2 garlic cloves, crushed
30cm/12in pizza base
8 slices of prosciutto
4 drained bottled artichoke hearts in oil, sliced
60ml/4 tbsp grated Parmesan cheese
salt and ground black pepper
fresh thyme sprigs, to garnish

SERVES 2–4

1 Preheat the oven to 220°C/425°F/Gas 7. Trim the spring onions, then chop all the white and a little of the green stems finely.

2 Heat 30ml/2 tbsp of the oil in a frying pan. Add the spring onions, mushrooms and garlic and fry over a moderately high heat for about 5 minutes until the mushrooms are golden and all the juices have evaporated. Add salt and pepper and leave to cool.

3 Brush the pizza base with half the remaining oil. Arrange the prosciutto and artichoke hearts to within 1cm/½in of the rim. Spoon the mushroom

mixture over the top. Sprinkle over the Parmesan, then drizzle with the remaining oil. Bake for 15–20 minutes or until the crust is crisp and golden. Garnish with thyme sprigs and serve at once.

Chicken, Shiitake Mushroom & Coriander Pizza

INGREDIENTS

45ml/3 tbsp olive oil
350g/12oz skinless, boneless chicken breasts, cut into thin strips
1 bunch spring onions, sliced
1 fresh red chilli, seeded and chopped
1 red pepper, seeded and cut into thin strips
75g/3oz fresh shiitake mushrooms, trimmed and sliced
45–60ml/3–4 tbsp chopped fresh coriander
30cm/12in pizza base
15ml/1 tbsp Chilli Oil
150g/5oz/scant 1 cup grated mozzarella cheese
salt and ground black pepper

SERVES 2–4

1 Preheat the oven to 220°C/425°F/Gas 7. Heat 30ml/2 tbsp of the olive oil in a wok or large frying pan. Add the chicken, spring onions, chilli, pepper and mushrooms. Stir-fry over a high heat for 2–3 minutes until the chicken is firm but still slightly pink inside. Add salt and pepper to taste.

2 Pour off any excess oil from the wok or frying pan. Allow the mixture to cool for 5 minutes, then stir in the chopped fresh coriander.

3 Brush the pizza base with the chilli oil. Spoon over the chicken and mushroom mixture to within 1cm/½in of the rim. Drizzle the remaining oil over the pizza.

4 Sprinkle the mozzarella over the pizza. Bake for 15–20 minutes or until the crust is crisp and golden. Serve at once.

Chorizo & Sweetcorn Pizza

INGREDIENTS

30cm/12in pizza base
15ml/1 tbsp Garlic Oil
1 quantity Tomato Sauce
175g/6oz chorizo sausages
50g/2oz/⅓ cup grated mozzarella cheese
30ml/2 tbsp grated Parmesan cheese
175g/6oz/1 cup drained canned sweetcorn
kernels
30ml/2 tbsp chopped fresh flat-leaf parsley

SERVES 2–4

1 Preheat the oven to 220°C/425°F/Gas 7. Brush the pizza base with garlic oil and spread over the tomato sauce to within 1cm/½in of the rim.

2 Skin the chorizo sausages, cut them into chunks and scatter them over the pizza base. Bake for 10 minutes. Meanwhile, mix together the mozzarella and Parmesan cheeses in a mixing bowl.

3 Then remove the pizza from the oven and sprinkle the sweetcorn and flat-leaf parsley over the top, followed by the mozzarella mixture. Return the pizza to the oven and bake for 5–10 minutes more until the crust is crisp and golden. Serve at once.

25

Pancetta, Leek & Smoked Mozzarella Pizzas

INGREDIENTS

2 leeks
30ml/2 tbsp grated Parmesan cheese
1 quantity Basic Pizza Dough
30ml/2 tbsp olive oil
8–12 slices of pancetta
150g/5oz/scant 1 cup grated smoked mozzarella cheese
ground black pepper

SERVES 4

26

1 Preheat the oven to 220°C/425°F/ Gas 7. Lightly grease two large baking sheets. Trim the leeks and slice them thinly. Wash them in a colander under cold running water and drain well.

2 Dust the work surface with the Parmesan, then knead it into the dough. Divide the dough into four pieces and roll each one out to a 13cm/5in round. Place well apart on the greased baking sheets, then push up the edge of the dough on each round to make a rim.

3 Brush half the oil over the pizza bases. Arrange the pancetta and leeks on top, then sprinkle over the grated smoked mozzarella cheese. Drizzle over the remaining oil and season with plenty of black pepper. Bake for 15–20 minutes or until the crust on each pizza is crisp and golden. Serve at once.

Caramelized Onion, Salami & Olive Pizza

INGREDIENTS

60ml/4 tbsp olive oil
675g/1½lb red onions, thinly sliced
12 stoned black olives, finely chopped
5ml/1 tsp dried herbes de Provence
1 quantity Basic Pizza Dough
6–8 slices of Italian salami, quartered
30–45ml/2–3 tbsp grated Parmesan cheese
ground black pepper

SERVES 4

28

2 On a lightly floured surface, knead the olives and herbs into the dough until evenly distributed. Roll out the dough and line a 30 x 18cm/12 x 7in Swiss roll tin. Push up the dough at the edges to make a thin rim all around. Brush the pizza base with half the remaining oil.

3 Spoon half of the caramelized onions over the pizza base. Cover them with the salami, then top with the remaining onions. Grind over plenty of black pepper and drizzle over the remaining oil.

4 Bake for 15–20 minutes or until the crust is crisp and golden. Remove from the oven and sprinkle the Parmesan over the pizza. Serve at once.

1 Preheat the oven to 220°C/425°F/ Gas 7. Heat 30ml/2 tbsp of the oil in a frying pan. Add the onions, stir once, then cover with foil or a lid. Cook

over a gentle heat for about 20 minutes, stirring occasionally, until the onions are soft and very lightly coloured. Leave to cool.

COOK'S TIP
If you are not keen on olives, use slivers of sun-dried tomatoes instead. Buy the type that are bottled in oil, drain them well, and use some of the oil for brushing the dough.

Ham & Pineapple French Bread Pizzas

INGREDIENTS

4 small baguettes
1 quantity Tomato Sauce
75g/3oz sliced cooked ham
4 drained canned pineapple rings, chopped
½ small green pepper, seeded and cut into thin strips
75g/3oz/¾ cup grated mature Cheddar cheese
salt and ground black pepper

SERVES 4

30

1 Preheat the oven to 200°C/400°F/Gas 6. Also preheat the grill. Cut the baguettes in half lengthways. Toast the cut sides under the grill until crisp and golden.

2 Then spread the tomato sauce over the toasted baguettes. Cut the ham into strips and arrange on top, with the pineapple chunks and green pepper  strips. Season with plenty of salt and pepper.

3 Sprinkle the grated Cheddar cheese evenly over the topped baguettes. Place on a lightly greased baking sheet and bake for 15–20 minutes until crisp and golden.

COOK'S TIP
You can save energy by grilling the French bread pizzas instead of baking them, if you prefer.

Smoked Chicken, Tomato & Pepper Pizzettes

INGREDIENTS

1 quantity Basic Pizza Dough
45ml / 3 tbsp olive oil
60ml / 4 tbsp sun-dried tomato paste
2 yellow peppers, seeded and cut into thin strips
175g / 6oz sliced smoked chicken or turkey, chopped
150g / 5oz / scant 1 cup diced mozzarella cheese
30ml / 2 tbsp shredded fresh basil
salt and ground black pepper

SERVES 4

1 Preheat the oven to 220°C/425°F/ Gas 7. Lightly grease two large baking sheets. Divide the dough into four pieces and roll each one out on a lightly  floured surface to a 13cm/5in round. Place well apart on the greased baking sheets, then push up the edge of the dough on each round to make a thin rim. Brush with 15ml/1 tbsp of the oil.

2 Spread the pizza bases generously with the sun-dried tomato paste. Heat half the remaining oil in a frying pan and stir-fry the pepper strips for about 4 minutes.  Arrange them on the pizza bases, with the smoked chicken or turkey.

3 Scatter over the mozzarella and basil. Season with plenty of salt and black pepper, then drizzle over the remaining oil. Bake for 15–20 minutes or until the crust on each pizzette is crisp and golden. Serve at once.

31

Pepperoni Pan Pizza

INGREDIENTS

115g/4oz/1 cup self-raising white flour
115g/4oz/1 cup self-raising wholemeal flour
pinch of salt
15ml/1 tbsp chopped fresh mixed herbs
50g/2oz/¼ cup butter, diced
about 150ml/¼ pint/⅔ cup milk
TOPPING
30ml/2 tbsp tomato purée
400g/14oz can chopped tomatoes, well drained
*50g/2oz/½ cup button mushrooms, thinly
sliced*
75g/3oz sliced pepperoni
6 stoned black olives, chopped
*115g/4oz/1 cup grated mature
Cheddar cheese*
15ml/1 tbsp shredded fresh basil, to garnish

SERVES 2–4

32

1 Grease a 22cm/8½in frying pan which can be used under the grill. Mix the flours, salt and herbs in a large bowl. Rub in the butter until the mixture resembles fine breadcrumbs. Mix in the milk very quickly to make a soft dough, then knead gently on a lightly floured surface until smooth. Roll out to fit the frying pan.

2 Cook the dough in the pan over a low heat for about 5 minutes, until the base is golden. Invert a baking sheet over the pan, then carefully flip the sheet and pan over to invert the pizza.

3 Slide the pizza base back into the pan, cooked side up. Spread over the tomato purée, then spoon the tomatoes on top. Scatter over the remaining ingredients and cook for 5 minutes more, until the underside of the pizza is golden. Preheat the grill.

4 Slide the pan under the grill and cook for about 5 minutes, until the cheese has melted and the topping is bubbling. Sprinkle the shredded fresh basil over the pizza and serve at once.

COOK'S TIP
*If you prefer, place the scone dough round on
a baking sheet, add the topping and bake it
in an oven preheated to 220°C/425°F/
Gas 7 for 20–25 minutes.*

Fish & Seafood
Pizzas

Prawn & Basil Pizzettes

INGREDIENTS

1 quantity Basic Pizza Dough
30ml/2 tbsp Chilli Oil
75g/3oz/½ cup grated mozzarella cheese
1 garlic clove, chopped
½ small red onion, thinly sliced
4–6 pieces of drained sun-dried tomatoes in oil, thinly sliced
115g/4oz cooked prawns, peeled and deveined
60ml/4 tbsp shredded fresh basil
salt and ground black pepper

SERVES 4

1 Preheat the oven to 220°C/425°F/Gas 7. Grease two large baking sheets. Pat out the dough to a thick round, then cut the round into eight equal-size wedges.

2 Roll out each wedge of dough on a lightly floured surface to a small oval, about 5mm/¼in thick. Place well apart on the greased baking sheets. Prick the dough all over with a fork.

3 Brush the pizza bases with 15ml/1 tbsp of the chilli oil. Top with the grated mozzarella cheese, leaving a clear 1cm/½in border all the way around the edge.

4 Divide the garlic, onion, sun-dried tomatoes, prawns and half the basil among the pizza bases. Add salt and pepper and drizzle the remaining chilli oil over the top. Bake for 8–10 minutes or until the crust on each pizzette is crisp and golden. Serve at once, sprinkled with the remaining basil.

35

Seafood Pizza

INGREDIENTS

450g/1lb peeled plum tomatoes or 2
400g/14oz cans chopped tomatoes, drained
175g/6oz small squid
225g/8oz fresh mussels
30cm/12in pizza base
175g/6oz raw or cooked prawns, peeled and
deveined
2 garlic cloves, finely chopped
45ml/3 tbsp chopped fresh parsley
30ml/2 tbsp olive oil
salt and ground black pepper

SERVES 4

1 Preheat the oven to 220°C/425°F/Gas 7. Strain the tomatoes through the medium holes of a food mill or sieve placed over a bowl, scraping in all the pulp. If you use canned tomatoes, drain them for at least 10 minutes before straining, or the topping will be too sloppy.

2 Prepare the squid by holding the body in one hand and gently pulling away the head and tentacles. Discard the head; chop the tentacles roughly. Keeping the body sac whole, remove the transparent "quill" from inside, then peel off the brown skin on the outside. Rinse the sac, rub with salt and rinse again. Drain, then slice into 5mm/¼in rings.

3 Carefully scrub the mussels, pulling off the beards and discarding any which are open. Place the mussels in a saucepan with a close-fitting lid. Add about 45ml/3 tbsp water. Close the pan tightly and shake over the heat until the mussels open. Transfer them to a dish, discarding any that remain closed.

4 Spread some of the puréed tomatoes on the pizza base to within 1cm/½in of the rim. Dot the prawns and the prepared squid evenly over the tomatoes. Sprinkle with the garlic and parsley. Season with plenty of salt and pepper, then drizzle with the olive oil.

5 Bake for 8 minutes, then remove from the oven and add the mussels on the half shell. Bake for 7–10 minutes more or until the crust is crisp and golden. Serve at once.

36

Mussel & Leek Pizzettes

INGREDIENTS

450g/1lb fresh mussels
120ml/4fl oz/½ cup dry white wine
1 quantity Basic Pizza Dough
15ml/1 tbsp olive oil
50g/2oz/½ cup grated Gruyère cheese
50g/2oz/½ cup grated mozzarella cheese
2 small leeks, sliced
salt and ground black pepper

SERVES 4

1 Preheat the oven to 220°C/425°F/Gas 7. Grease two large baking sheets. Carefully scrub the mussels, pull off the beards and discard any which are open. Place the mussels in a pan.

2 Add the dry white wine, close the pan lid tightly and shake over the heat until the mussels open. Transfer the mussels to a dish, discarding any that remain closed, then remove them from their shells and leave them to cool.

3 Divide the dough into four pieces and roll each one out on a lightly floured surface to a 13cm/5in round. Place well apart on the greased baking sheets, then push up the edge of the dough on each round to make a thin rim. Brush the bases with the oil and sprinkle with half the mixed cheeses.

4 Scatter the leeks over the cheese. Bake for 10 minutes, then arrange the mussels on top of the pizzettes. Season with salt and pepper. Sprinkle with the remaining mixed cheeses and bake for 5–10 minutes more, until the crust on each pizzette is crisp and golden. Serve at once.

Anchovy, Pepper & Tomato Pizza

INGREDIENTS

6 plum tomatoes
45ml/3 tbsp olive oil
5ml/1 tsp salt
1 large red pepper
1 large yellow pepper
30cm/12in pizza base
2 garlic cloves, chopped
50g/2oz can anchovy fillets, drained
ground black pepper
fresh basil leaves, to garnish

SERVES 2–4

1 Cut the tomatoes in half lengthways and scoop out the seeds. Chop the flesh roughly and place it in a bowl. Add 15ml/1 tbsp of the oil and the salt. Mix well, then cover and leave to marinate for 30 minutes.

2 Meanwhile, preheat the oven to 220°C/425°F/ Gas 7, and the grill to high. Slice the peppers in half lengthways and remove the core and seeds. Arrange the pepper halves, skin side up, on a baking sheet. Grill until the skins are evenly charred.

3 Place the peppers in a heatproof bowl. Cover with several layers of kitchen paper and leave for 10–15 minutes. Peel off the pepper skins and cut the flesh into thin strips.

4 Brush the pizza base with half the remaining oil. Drain the marinated tomatoes and scatter them over the base to within 1cm/½in of the pizza rim. Arrange the peppers and garlic evenly over the pizza base.

5 Snip up the anchovy fillets into small pieces and sprinkle them over the pizza base. Season with ground black pepper. Drizzle over the remaining oil and bake for 15–20 minutes or until the crust is crisp and golden. Serve at once, garnished with the whole fresh basil leaves.

Tuna, Anchovy & Caper Scone Pizza

INGREDIENTS

115g/4oz/1 cup self-raising white flour
115g/4oz/1 cup self-raising wholemeal flour
pinch of salt
50g/2oz/¼ cup butter, diced
about 150ml/¼ pint/⅔ cup milk
TOPPING
30ml/2 tbsp olive oil
1 quantity Tomato Sauce
1 small red onion, cut in thin wedges
200g/7oz can tuna, drained and flaked
15ml/1 tbsp drained capers
12 stoned black olives
45ml/3 tbsp grated Parmesan cheese
50g/2oz can anchovy fillets, drained and
halved lengthways
ground black pepper

SERVES 2–4

1 Preheat the oven to 220°C/425°F/Gas 7. Mix the flours and salt in a large bowl. Rub in the butter until the mixture resembles fine breadcrumbs. Mix in the milk very quickly to make a soft dough, then knead gently on a lightly floured surface and roll out to a 25cm/10in round.

2 Brush the scone dough base with 15ml/1 tbsp of the oil. Spread the tomato sauce to within 1cm/½in of the rim, then arrange the onion wedges and flaked tuna on top. Dot with the capers and olives, then sprinkle with the Parmesan.

3 Make a lattice with the anchovy fillets on top of the pizza. Drizzle over the remaining oil and add a generous grinding of black pepper. Bake in the preheated  oven for 15–20 minutes or until the scone crust is crisp and golden. Serve at once.

42

Salmon & Avocado Pizza

INGREDIENTS

150g/5oz salmon fillet
120ml/4fl oz/½ cup white wine
30cm/12in pizza base
15ml/1 tbsp olive oil
400g/14oz can chopped tomatoes, well drained
115g/4oz/⅔ cup grated mozzarella cheese
1 small avocado
10ml/2 tsp lemon juice
30ml/2 tbsp crème fraîche
75g/3oz smoked salmon, cut into strips
15ml/1 tbsp drained capers
30ml/2 tbsp snipped fresh chives, to garnish
ground black pepper

SERVES 2–4

1 Preheat the oven to 220°C/425°F/ Gas 7. Place the salmon fillet in a frying pan, pour over the wine and season with black pepper. Bring slowly to the boil, remove the pan from the heat, cover and let the fish finish cooking in the cooling liquid. Skin the salmon and flake it finely, removing any bones.

2 Brush the pizza base with the oil and spread the drained tomatoes over the base to within 1cm/½in of the rim. Sprinkle over half the grated mozzarella. Bake for 10 minutes.

3 Meanwhile, cut the avocado in half. Lift out the stone, remove the peel and slice the flesh into small cubes. Toss with the lemon juice in a bowl.

4 Remove the pizza from the oven, dot with crème fraîche and arrange the fresh and smoked salmon on top. Add the drained avocado cubes, capers and remaining mozzarella, with black pepper. Bake for 5–10 minutes more or until the crust is crisp and golden. Sprinkle with the chives and serve at once.

43

Vegetarian Pizzas

Fresh Vegetable Pizza

INGREDIENTS

450g/1lb peeled plum tomatoes or 2
400g/14oz cans chopped tomatoes, drained
3 small courgettes, trimmed
2 broccoli spears, broken into small florets
225g/8oz fresh asparagus spears, trimmed and
cut into short lengths
45ml/3 tbsp olive oil
50g/2oz/½ cup shelled peas, fresh or
thawed frozen
4 spring onions, sliced
30cm/12in pizza base
75g/3oz/½ cup diced mozzarella cheese
10 fresh basil leaves, torn into pieces
2 garlic cloves, finely chopped
salt and ground black pepper

SERVES 2–4

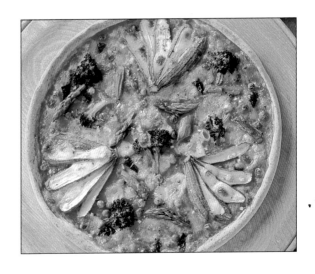

1 Preheat the oven to 220°C/425°F/Gas 7. Strain the tomatoes through the medium holes of a food mill or sieve placed over a bowl, scraping in all the pulp. If you use canned tomatoes, drain them for at least 10 minutes before straining, or the topping will be too sloppy.

2 Slice the courgettes lengthways, keeping them intact at one end. Bring a saucepan of lightly salted water to the boil, add the broccoli, asparagus and courgettes and blanch for 4–5 minutes. Drain well.

3 Heat 30ml/2 tbsp of the olive oil in a saucepan. Stir-fry the peas and spring onions for 5 minutes. Spread the puréed tomatoes over the pizza base to within 1cm/½in of the rim. Arrange the blanched and stir-fried vegetables on top, fanning out the courgettes.

4 Sprinkle with the mozzarella, basil, garlic, salt and pepper. Drizzle the remaining oil over the top and bake for 15–20 minutes or until the crust is crisp and golden. Serve at once.

Roasted Vegetable & Goat's Cheese Pizza

INGREDIENTS

1 aubergine, cut into thick chunks
2 small courgettes, sliced lengthways
1 red pepper, quartered and seeded
1 yellow pepper, quartered and seeded
1 small red onion, cut into wedges
90ml/6 tbsp Garlic Oil
1 goat's cheese, about 115g/4oz
30cm/12in pizza base
400g/14oz can chopped tomatoes, well drained
15ml/1 tbsp chopped fresh thyme
ground black pepper
green olive tapenade, to serve

SERVES 2–4

1 Preheat the oven to 220°C/425°F/ Gas 7. Place the aubergine, courgette slices, peppers and onion in a large roasting tin. (The peppers should be skin-side up.) Brush with 60ml/4 tbsp of the garlic oil. Roast for 30 minutes until lightly charred, turning the peppers over halfway through cooking.

2 Meanwhile, without removing the rind, cut the goat's cheese into cubes. Remove the roasting tin from the oven. Transfer the peppers to a bowl, cover with several layers of kitchen paper and leave for 10–15 minutes.

3 Peel the skins from the peppers and cut the flesh into thick strips. Brush the pizza base with half the remaining garlic oil and spread the drained chopped tomatoes over the base to within 1cm/½ in of the rim. Arrange the roasted vegetables and goat's cheese on top.

4 Then scatter the chopped thyme over the pizza and drizzle with the remaining garlic oil. Season with a generous grinding of black pepper. Bake in the preheated oven for 15–20 minutes or until the crust is crisp and golden. Spoon over the green olive tapenade and serve at once.

46

Fresh Herb & Garlic Pizza

INGREDIENTS

115g/4oz/2 cups fresh mixed herbs, such as parsley, basil and oregano
3 garlic cloves, crushed
120ml/4fl oz/½ cup double cream
30cm/12in pizza base
15ml/1 tbsp Garlic Oil
115g/4oz/1 cup grated Pecorino cheese
salt and ground black pepper

SERVES 4

48

1 Preheat the oven to 220°C/425°F/ Gas 7. Place the mixed herbs on a board and chop with a mezzaluna. Alternatively, you can pulse the herbs in a food processor, but be careful not to allow them to form a paste.

2 Tip the herbs into a mixing bowl and add the garlic and cream. Season with plenty of salt and pepper, then mix well.

3 Brush the pizza base with the garlic oil, then spread the herb mixture over the top to within 1cm/½ in of the rim. Sprinkle over the Pecorino.

4 Bake the pizza in the oven for 15–20 minutes or until the crust is crisp and golden. Serve at once.

COOK'S TIP

This pizza makes a wonderfully flavoursome cocktail snack. Cut the pizza into eight thin wedges before serving.

Wild Mushroom Pizzettes

INGREDIENTS

45ml/3 tbsp olive oil
350g/12oz/3 cups fresh wild mushrooms,
washed and sliced
2 shallots, chopped
2 garlic cloves, crushed
30ml/2 tbsp chopped fresh mixed thyme and
flat-leaf parsley
1 quantity Basic Pizza Dough
50g/2oz/½ cup grated Gruyère cheese
30ml/2 tbsp grated Parmesan cheese
salt and ground black pepper

SERVES 4

2 Divide the dough into four pieces and roll each one out on a lightly floured surface to a 13cm/5in round. Place on the greased baking sheets, then push up the edge of the dough on each round to make a thin rim.

3 Brush the pizzette bases with the remaining oil and top with the mushroom mixture. Mix the Gruyère and Parmesan cheeses and sprinkle them over. Bake for 15–20 minutes or until the crust on each pizzette is crisp and golden. Sprinkle with the remaining herbs and serve at once.

49

1 Preheat the oven to 220°C/425°F/ Gas 7. Grease two large baking sheets. Heat 30ml/2 tbsp of the oil in a frying pan. Add the mushrooms, shallots and garlic and  cook over a moderately high heat for about 5 minutes, until the mushrooms are golden and most of the juices have evaporated. Stir in half the herbs, with salt and pepper to taste. Leave to cool.

Tomato, Pesto & Black Olive Pizzettes

INGREDIENTS

2 plum tomatoes
1 garlic clove, crushed
60ml/4 tbsp olive oil
1 quantity Basic Pizza Dough
30ml/2 tbsp red pesto
150g/5oz mozzarella cheese, thinly sliced
4 stoned black olives, chopped
15ml/1 tbsp chopped fresh oregano
salt and ground black pepper
fresh oregano leaves, to garnish

SERVES 4

1 Cut the tomatoes in half, then slice them thinly. Place the tomatoes and the crushed garlic in a shallow bowl, drizzle over 30ml/2 tbsp of the oil and sprinkle with salt and pepper. Leave to marinate for 15 minutes.

2 Preheat the oven to 220°C/425°F/Gas 7. Grease two large baking sheets. Divide the dough into four pieces and roll each one out on a lightly floured surface to a 13cm/5in round. Place the bases well apart on the greased baking sheets, then push up the edge of the dough on each base to make a thin rim.

3 Then brush the pizzette bases with half the remaining oil and spread over the red pesto. Drain the tomatoes and arrange a fan of alternate slices of tomatoes and mozzarella on each base.

4 Dot the pizzettes with the olives and sprinkle with the chopped oregano. Drizzle with the remaining oil and bake for 15–20 minutes or until the crust on each pizzette is crisp and golden. Garnish with the whole fresh oregano leaves and serve at once.

Red Onion & Gorgonzola Pizza Bites

INGREDIENTS

1 quantity Basic Pizza Dough
30ml/2 tbsp Garlic Oil
2 small red onions, halved, then sliced into thin wedges
150g/5oz Gorgonzola piccante
2 garlic cloves, cut into thin slivers
10ml/2 tsp chopped fresh sage
ground black pepper

SERVES 4

1 Preheat the oven to 220°C/425°F/ Gas 7. Lightly grease two baking sheets. Divide the pizza dough into eight pieces and roll out each piece to a small oval about 5mm/¼in thick. Place the pizza bases well apart on the greased baking sheets and prick them all over with a fork. Brush the bases with 15ml/1 tbsp of the garlic oil.

2 Then scatter the onion wedges over the bases. Remove the rind from the Gorgonzola and cut the cheese into small cubes. Scatter the Gorgonzola cubes over the onion wedges.

3 Sprinkle the garlic slivers over the Gorgonzola cubes, with the chopped fresh sage. Drizzle over the remaining oil. Add a generous grinding of black pepper and bake for 15–20 minutes or until the crust is crisp and golden. Serve at once.

Onion & Three Cheese Pizza

INGREDIENTS

45ml/3 tbsp olive oil
3 onions, sliced
30cm/12in pizza base
4 small tomatoes, peeled, seeded and cut into thin wedges
30ml/2 tbsp shredded fresh basil
115g/4oz Dolcelatte cheese
150g/5oz mozzarella cheese
115g/4oz Red Leicester cheese
ground black pepper
fresh basil leaves, to garnish

SERVES 4

2 Brush the pizza base with the remaining oil. Spoon over the onions and tomatoes, then scatter the shredded basil over the top.

3 Slice the cheeses thinly and arrange the slices over the tomatoes and the onions. Add a generous grinding of black pepper. Bake for 15–20 minutes or until the crust is crisp and golden. Sprinkle with fresh basil leaves to garnish and serve at once.

1 Preheat the oven to 220°C/425°F/ Gas 7. Heat 30ml/2 tbsp of the oil in a frying pan. Add the onions and fry over a gentle heat for about 10 min-

utes, stirring occasionally, until the onions are soft. Leave to cool.

Feta, Roasted Garlic & Oregano Pizzettes

INGREDIENTS

1 garlic bulb
45ml/3 tbsp olive oil
1 red pepper, quartered and seeded
1 yellow pepper, quartered and seeded
1 quantity Basic Pizza Dough
2 plum tomatoes, peeled, seeded and chopped
175g/6oz/1 cup feta cheese, crumbled
ground black pepper
15–30ml/1–2 tbsp shredded fresh oregano, to garnish

SERVES 4

1 Preheat the oven to 220°C/425°F/Gas 7 and also the grill to high. Grease two large baking sheets. Break the garlic into cloves, discarding the papery outer layers, but leaving the skin on the cloves. Put them in a bowl and toss with 15ml/1 tbsp of the oil.

2 Grill the peppers, skin-side up, until the skins are evenly charred. Place them in a heatproof bowl. Cover with several layers of kitchen paper and leave for 10–15 minutes. Peel off the pepper skins and cut the flesh into thin strips.

3 Divide the dough into four pieces and roll each one out on a lightly floured surface to a 13cm/5in round. Place the rounds well apart on the greased baking sheets, then push up the edge of the dough on each round to make a thin rim.

4 Brush over half the remaining oil and scatter over the chopped tomatoes. Top with the peppers, feta and garlic cloves. Drizzle over the remaining oil and season with black pepper. Bake for 15–20 minutes or until the crust on each pizzette is crisp and golden. Garnish with the oregano and serve at once.

Party Pizzas

Smoked Salmon Pizzettes

INGREDIENTS

15ml/1 tbsp finely snipped fresh chives
1 quantity Basic Pizza Dough
15ml/1 tbsp olive oil
75–115g/3–4oz smoked salmon,
cut into strips
60ml/4 tbsp crème fraîche
30ml/2 tbsp black lumpfish roe
halved fresh chives, to garnish

MAKES 10–12

1 Preheat the oven to 200°C/400°F/ Gas 6. Lightly grease two large baking sheets. On a lightly floured surface, knead the finely snipped chives into the pizza dough until they are evenly distributed. Roll out the dough to a thickness of about 3mm/⅛in. Using a 7.5cm/3in plain round cutter, stamp out 10–12 rounds.

2 Place the pizzette bases well apart on the greased baking sheets. Prick them all over with a fork, then brush with the olive oil. Bake for 10–12 minutes, until each base is crisp and golden.

3 Arrange the strips of smoked salmon on top of the pizzettes, folding them to avoid overlapping the edges. Place a spoonful of crème fraîche in the centre of each pizzette and add a tiny amount of lumpfish roe in the centre. Garnish with the fresh chives and serve at once.

55

Spinach & Ricotta Panzerotti

INGREDIENTS

*115g/4oz frozen chopped spinach, thawed,
drained and squeezed dry
50g/2oz/¼ cup ricotta cheese
50g/2oz/⅓ cup grated Parmesan cheese
generous pinch of grated nutmeg
double quantity Basic Pizza Dough
1 egg white, lightly beaten
vegetable oil, for deep-frying
salt and ground black pepper*

MAKES 20–24

1 Mix the spinach, ricotta, Parmesan and nutmeg in a bowl. Stir in salt and pepper to taste, then beat until smooth.

2 Roll out the dough on a lightly floured surface to a thickness of about 3mm/⅛in. Using a 7.5cm/ 3in plain cutter, stamp out 20–24 rounds. Spread  about a teaspoon of spinach mixture on one half of each circle, leaving the outer rim clear.

3 Brush the edges of the dough with a little egg white, fold the uncovered half of each round of dough over the filling and press the edges firmly together to seal.

4 Heat the oil for deep-frying in a large saucepan or deep-fryer. Add the panzerotti, a few at a time, and deep-fry for about 3 minutes, until they are crisp  and golden. Remove them from the pan with a slotted spoon and drain on kitchen paper. Keep the cooked panzerotti hot while deep-frying the subsequent batches, but do not leave them for too long before serving; they are at their best when freshly fried.

VARIATION
Chop five drained artichoke hearts finely and use them instead of the spinach for an unusual and very tasty filling.

56

Quick Party Pizza Bites

INGREDIENTS

115g/4oz/1 cup self-raising white flour
115g/4oz/1 cup self-raising wholemeal flour
pinch of salt
50g/2oz/¼ cup butter, diced
10 fresh basil leaves, plus extra to garnish
about 150ml/¼ pint/⅔ cup milk
TOPPING
115g/4oz/⅔ cup drained sun-dried tomatoes
in oil, chopped, plus 30ml/2 tbsp
oil from jar
1 quantity Tomato Sauce
10 stoned black olives, chopped
15ml/1 tbsp shredded fresh basil
50g/2oz/½ cup grated mozzarella cheese
30ml/2 tbsp grated Parmesan cheese

MAKES 24

1 Preheat the oven to 220°C/425°F/Gas 7. Mix the flours and salt in a large bowl. Rub in the butter until the mixture resembles fine breadcrumbs. Tear the basil leaves roughly, then add them to the mixture. Mix in the milk quickly to make a soft dough.

2 Knead the dough gently on a lightly floured surface until smooth. Roll out and line a 30 x 18cm/ 12 x 7in Swiss roll tin. Push up the edges to make a thin rim.

3 Brush the base with 15ml/1 tbsp of the tomato oil, then spread over the tomato sauce. Scatter the sun-dried tomatoes and olives over the top, with the shredded basil.

4 Mix the cheeses in a bowl, then sprinkle them over the pizza base. Drizzle over the remaining tomato oil. Bake for about 20 minutes in the preheated oven. Cut into 24 bite-size pieces, garnish with extra shredded basil leaves and serve at once.

Mini Pizzas with Mozzarella, Anchovy & Pesto

INGREDIENTS

*2 ready-to-cook pizza bases, about 20cm/8in
in diameter
60ml/4 tbsp olive oil
30ml/2 tbsp red pesto
12 stoned black olives
75g/3oz/½ cup diced mozzarella cheese
50g/2oz/⅓ cup drained sun-dried tomatoes
in oil, chopped
30–45ml/2–3 tbsp drained capers
50g/2oz can anchovy fillets, drained and
roughly chopped
30ml/2 tbsp grated Parmesan cheese
fresh parsley sprigs, to garnish*

MAKES 24

1 Preheat the oven to 220°C/425°F/Gas 7. Grease two large baking sheets. Using a 5cm/2in plain round cutter, stamp out 24 rounds from the pizza bases and arrange them on the baking sheets. Brush the bases with 30ml/2 tbsp of the oil, then spread with the pesto.

2 Cut the olives lengthways into quarters. Arrange on top of the pizza bases, with the mozzarella, sun-dried tomatoes, capers and anchovies.

3 Sprinkle over the Parmesan, then drizzle with the remaining oil. Bake for 8–10 minutes or until the crust on each mini pizza is crisp and golden. Garnish with fresh parsley sprigs and serve at once.

COOK'S TIP

If you are in a hurry, just add the topping to the whole pizza bases. When cooked, cut them into slender wedges for serving.

Tomato & Basil Tart

INGREDIENTS

175g/6oz/1½ cups plain flour
2.5ml/½ tsp salt
115g/4oz/½ cup butter or margarine, chilled
45–75ml/3–5 tbsp cold water
TOPPING
30ml/2 tbsp extra-virgin olive oil
175g/6oz mozzarella cheese, very thinly sliced
12 fresh basil leaves
4–5 tomatoes, sliced
60ml/4 tbsp grated Parmesan cheese
salt and ground black pepper

SERVES 6–8

1 Mix the flour and salt in a large bowl. Rub in the butter or margarine until the mixture resembles fine breadcrumbs, then add just enough water to bind the dough. Gather the pastry into a ball, flatten it to a disc and wrap in greaseproof paper. Chill for 40 minutes.

2 Preheat the oven to 190°C/375°F/Gas 5. Roll out the pastry on a lightly floured surface and line a 28cm/11in pie tin or pizza pan. Trim the edges evenly. Chill for 10 minutes if you have time.

3 Line the pastry with greaseproof paper and baking beans. Bake blind for 15 minutes, then remove the pastry case from the oven and lift out the paper and beans. Leave the oven on for baking the filled tart.

4 Brush the pastry case with a little of the oil and arrange the mozzarella slices over the surface. Shred half the basil leaves and sprinkle them over the mozzarella, then arrange the tomato slices in concentric circles on top.

5 Dot the surface with the remaining whole basil leaves. Sprinkle with salt and pepper. Spoon the Parmesan over the top and drizzle with the remaining oil. Bake for 35 minutes. Serve hot or at room temperature.

COOK'S TIP
If the melted cheese exudes a lot of liquid during baking, tilt the tin and spoon it off to prevent the pastry from becoming soggy.

Farmhouse Pizza

INGREDIENTS

75ml/5 tbsp olive oil
225g/8oz/2 cups button mushrooms, sliced
double quantity Basic Pizza Dough
1 quantity Tomato Sauce
275g/10oz mozzarella cheese, thinly sliced
115g/4oz wafer-thin smoked ham slices
6 drained bottled artichoke hearts in oil, sliced
*50g/2oz can anchovy fillets, drained and
halved lengthways*
10 stoned black olives, halved
30ml/2 tbsp chopped fresh oregano
45ml/3 tbsp grated Parmesan cheese
ground black pepper

SERVES 4–6

1 Preheat the oven to 220°C/425°F/ Gas 7. Lightly grease a 30 x 25cm/12 x 10in baking sheet. Heat 30ml/2 tbsp of the oil in a large frying pan. Add  the mushrooms and cook over a moderately high heat for about 5 minutes, until they are golden and most of the juices have evaporated. Leave to cool.

2 Knead the dough gently on a lightly floured surface until smooth. Roll out to fit the greased baking sheet, then push up the dough edges to make a thin rim. Brush with 30ml/2 tbsp of the oil, then spread with the tomato sauce.

3 Arrange the mozzarella slices over the tomato sauce. Scrunch up the smoked ham slices and arrange on top, with the artichoke hearts, mushrooms and  anchovies. Dot with the halved black olives.

4 Sprinkle the chopped fresh oregano and Parmesan cheese over the top of the pizza. Drizzle over the remaining oil and season with plenty of black pepper. Bake for about 25 minutes or until the crust is crisp and golden. Serve at once.

COOK'S TIP

For a special treat, try this pizza with wild mushrooms and prosciutto instead of the button mushrooms and smoked ham.

62

Index